PIANO | VOCAL | GUITAR

BEST OF
COUNT BASIE

Cover photo © Michael Ochs Archives/Getty Images

ISBN 978-1-4768-6796-0

HAL•LEONARD®
CORPORATION

7777 W. BLUEMOUND RD. P.O. BOX 13819 MILWAUKEE, WI 53213

Visit Hal Leonard Online at
www.halleonard.com

AFTER YOU'VE GONE

Words by HENRY CREAMER
Music by TURNER LAYTON

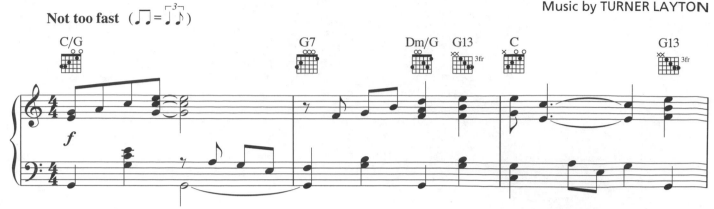

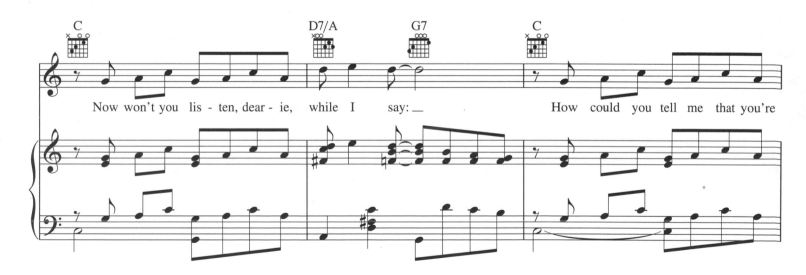

Now won't you lis-ten, dear-ie, while I say: ___ How could you tell me that you're

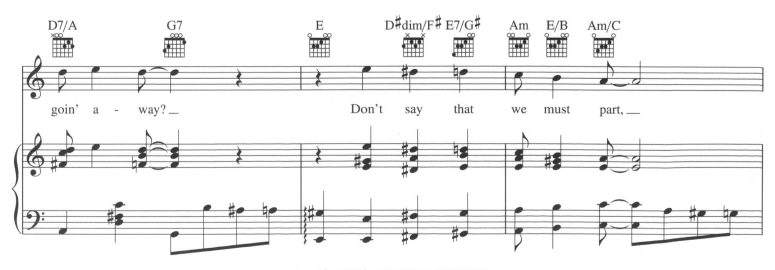

goin' a-way? ___ Don't say that we must part, ___

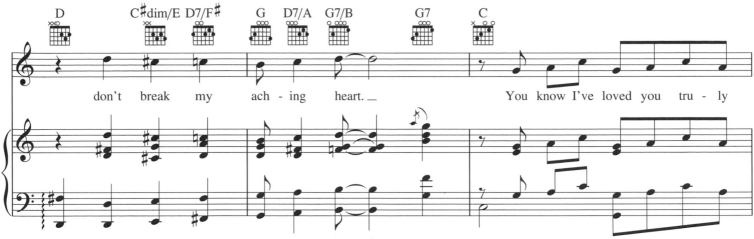

don't break my ach-ing heart. ___ You know I've loved you tru-ly

man-y years, ___ loved you night and day. ___

How can you leave me, can't you see my tears? ___ Lis-ten while ___ I

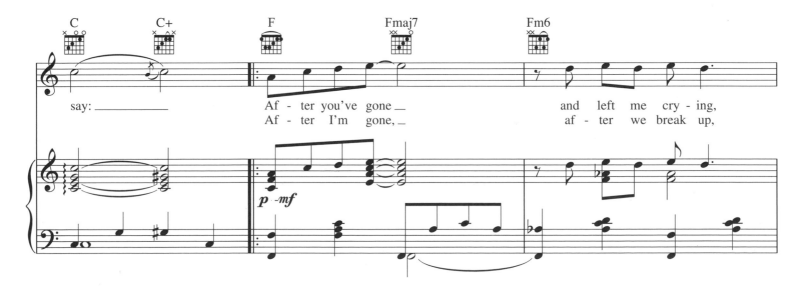

say: _____

Af-ter you've gone ___ and left me cry-ing,
Af-ter I'm gone, ___ af-ter we break up,

p - mf

there'll come a time, _ when you'll re-gret it. Some - day,
their joy and tears, _ all kinds of weath-er, some - day,

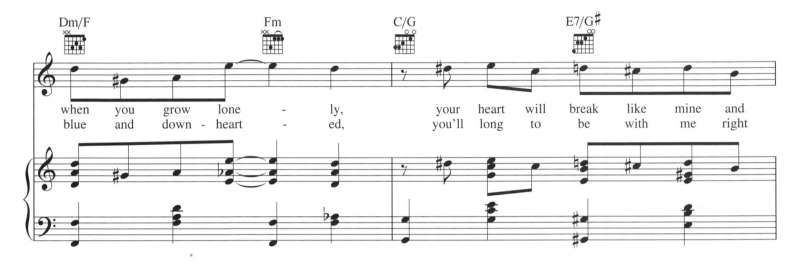

when you grow lone - ly, your heart will break like mine and
blue and down-heart - ed, you'll long to be with me right

you'll want me on - ly, af - ter you've gone, _ af - ter you've gone a -
back where you start - ed; af - ter I'm gone, _ af - ter I'm gone a -

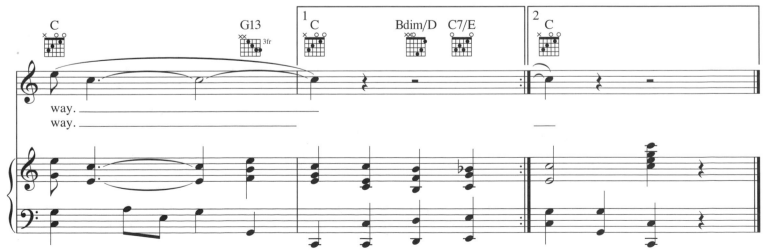

way. _____
way. _____

APRIL IN PARIS

Words by E.Y. "YIP" HARBURG
Music by VERNON DUKE

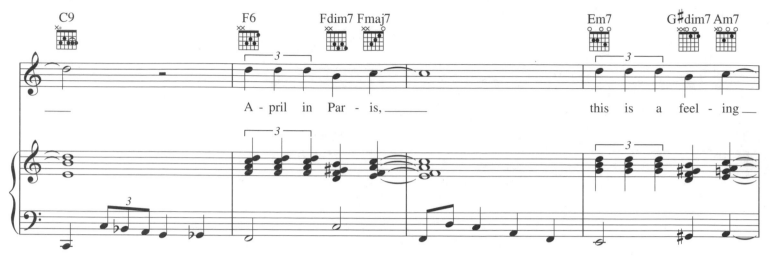

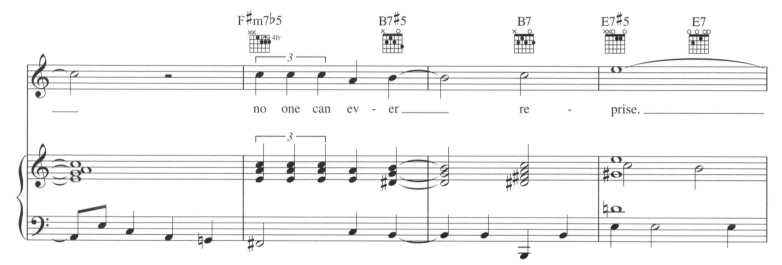

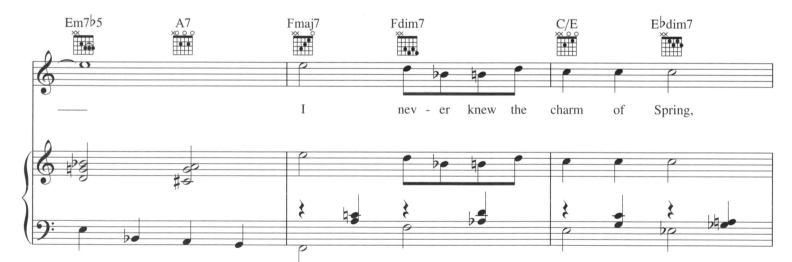

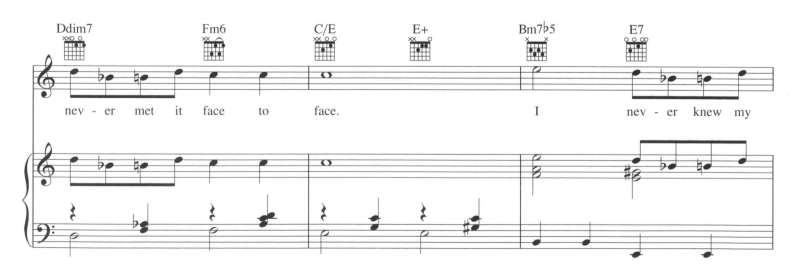

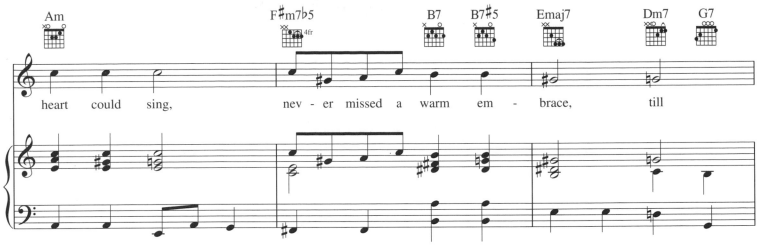

heart could sing, never missed a warm em - brace, till

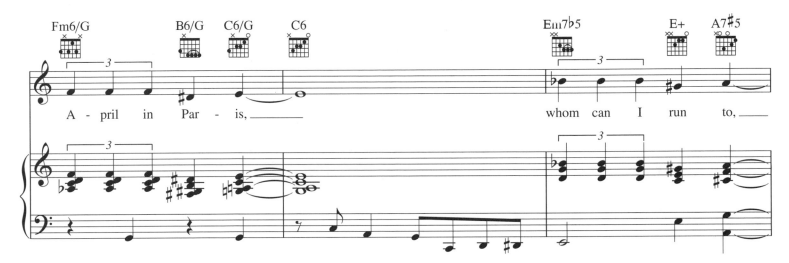

A - pril in Par - is, whom can I run to,

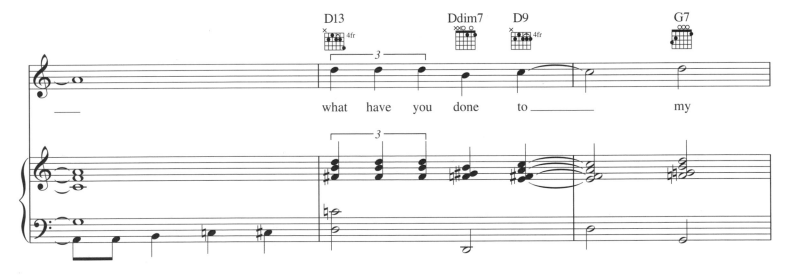

what have you done to my

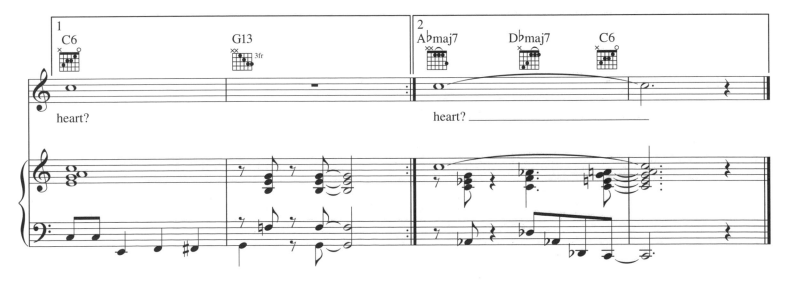

heart?

heart?

BASIE BOOGIE

By COUNT BASIE
and MILTON EBBINS

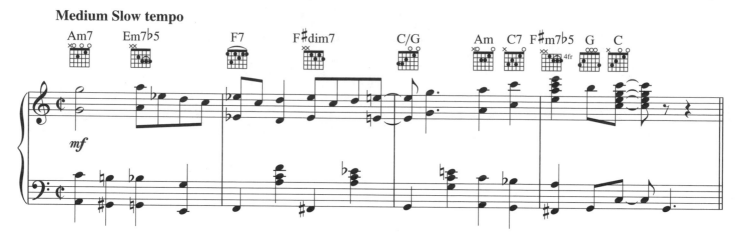

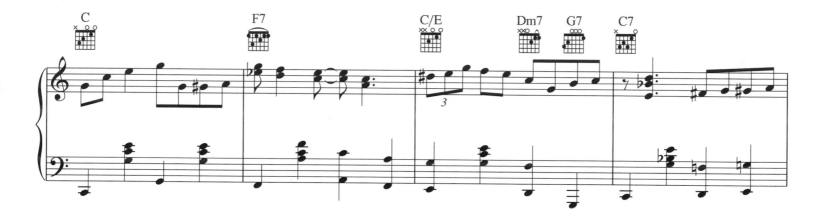

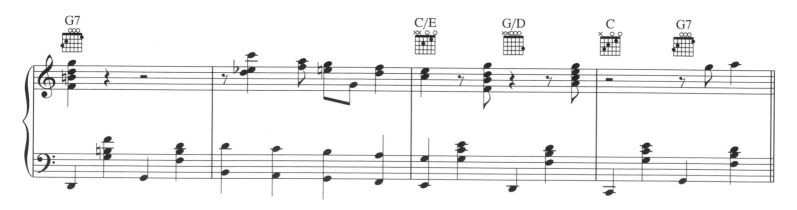

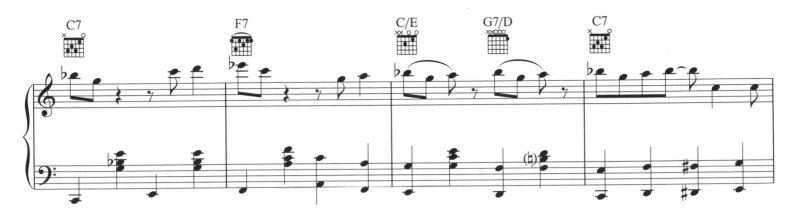

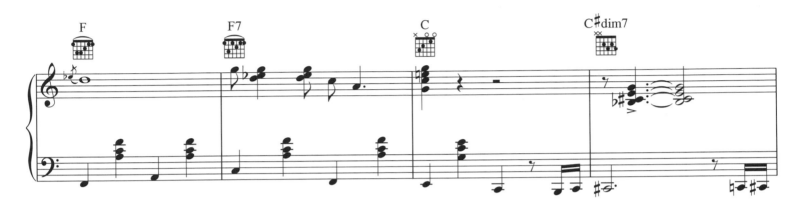

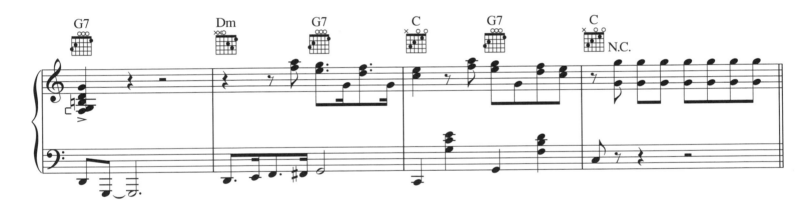

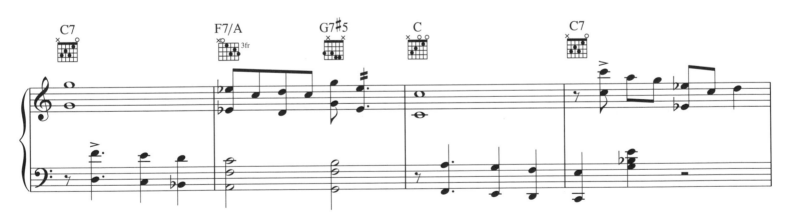

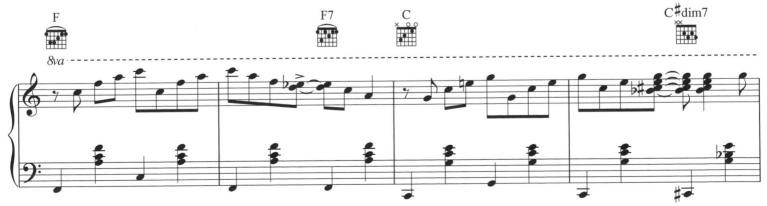

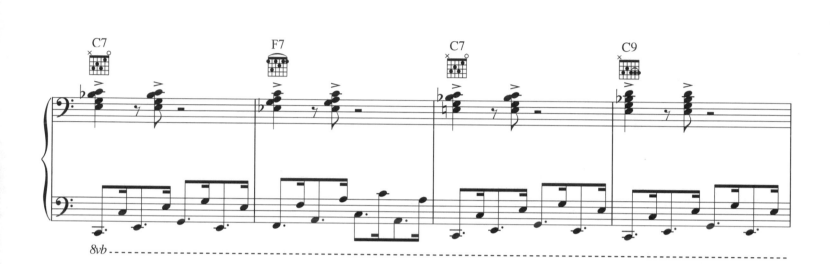

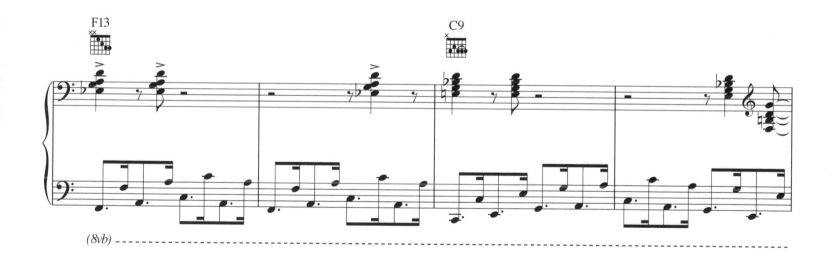

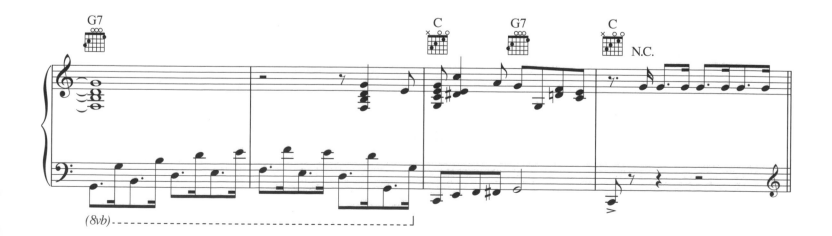

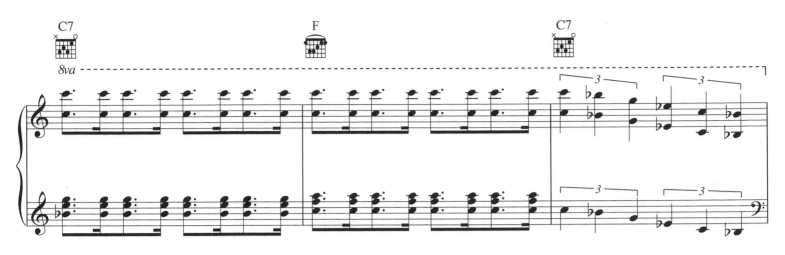

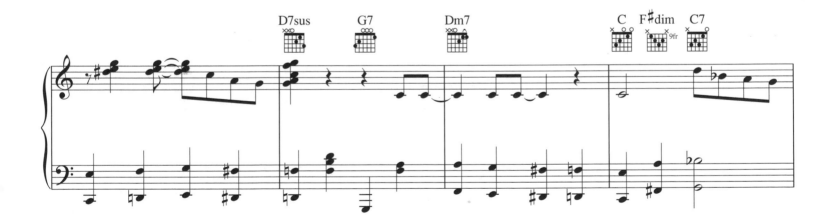

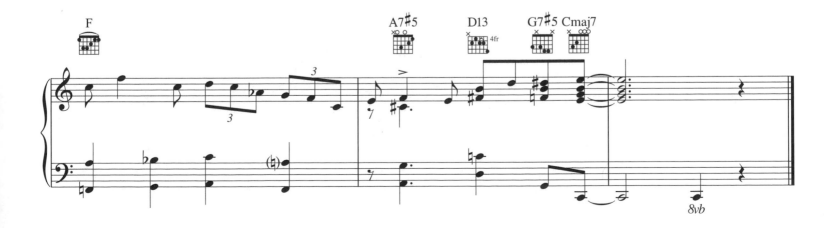

BLUE AND SENTIMENTAL

Words and Music by COUNT BASIE,
JERRY LIVINGSTON and MACK DAVID

The ro-mance is o - ver, you've bro-ken each vow.

You nev-er loved me, I see it all now. I should be glad that we're through,

but I'm still in love with you.

Slowly, with a lift

Blue and sen - ti - men - tal, my dreams are blue dreams. Just won't come true dreams, I

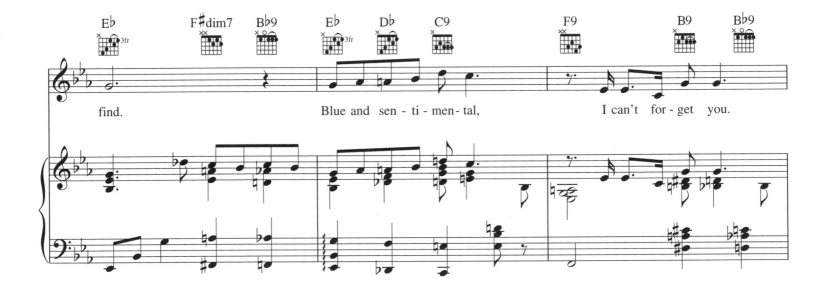

find. Blue and sen - ti - men - tal, I can't for - get you.

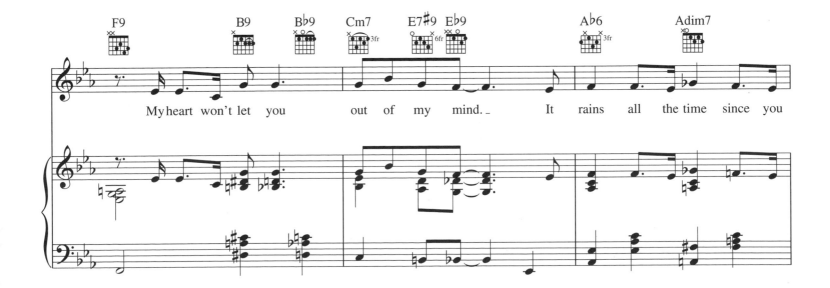

My heart won't let you out of my mind. __ It rains all the time since you

said, "Good - bye." __ The skies, and my eyes, and my heart all cry. __

Blue and sen - ti - men - tal, if you don't want me, why do you haunt me and

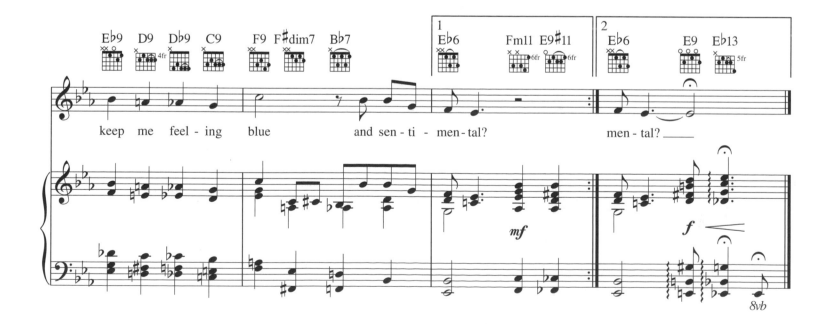

keep me feel - ing blue and sen - ti - men - tal? men - tal? ____

8vb

CUTE

Music by NEAL HEFTI
Lyrics by STANLEY STYNE

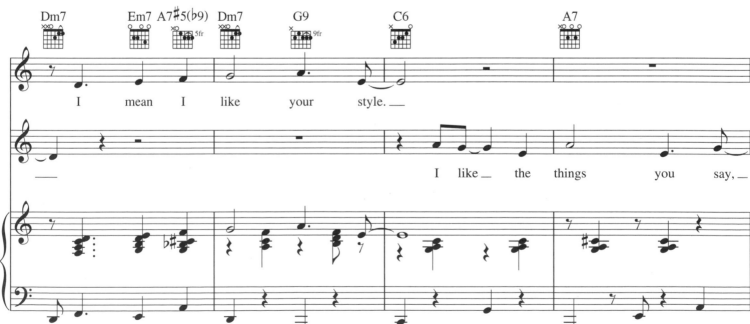

EVERY DAY I HAVE THE BLUES

Words and Music by
PETER CHATMAN

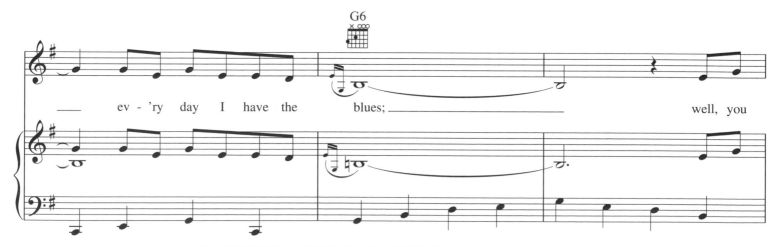

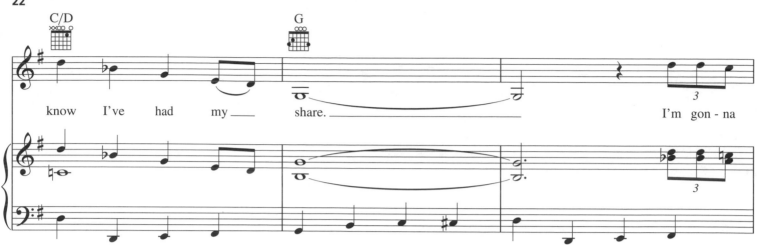

know I've had my ___ share. ___ I'm gon - na

pack my suit-case, ___ mov-in' on down the line, ___

___ oh, ___ I'm ___ gon-na pack my suit-case, move on down the

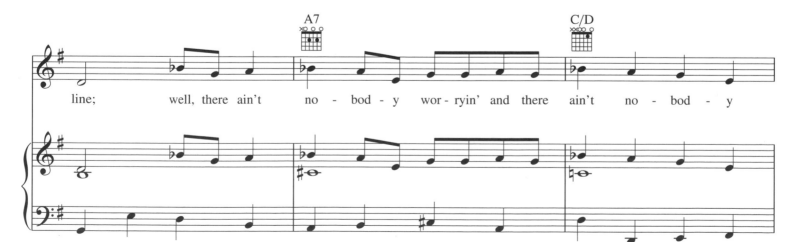

line; well, there ain't no-bod-y wor-ryin' and there ain't no-bod-y

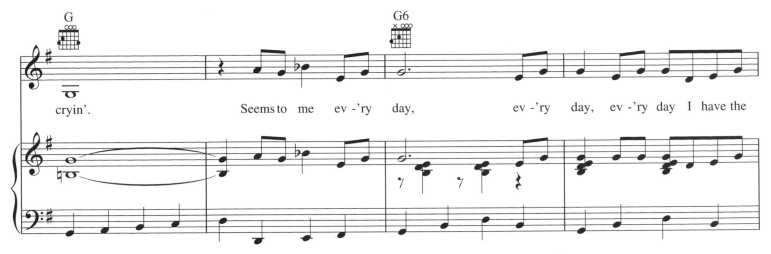

cryin'. Seems to me ev-'ry day, ev-'ry day, ev-'ry day I have the

blues, _____ ev-'ry day, ev-'ry day, ev-'ry day, ev-'ry day I have the

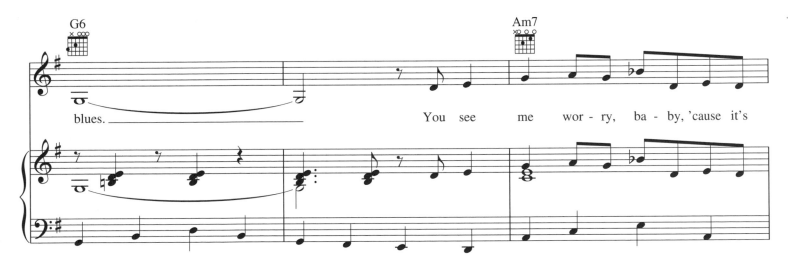

blues. _____ You see me wor-ry, ba-by, 'cause it's

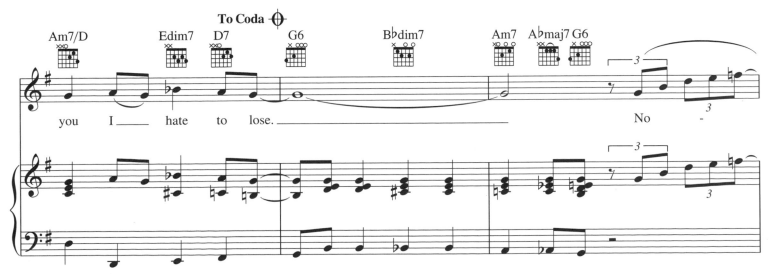

you I ___ hate to lose. _____ No -

-bod-y loves me, no - bod-y seems to care; __

__ no - bod-y loves me, no - bod-y seems to care; __

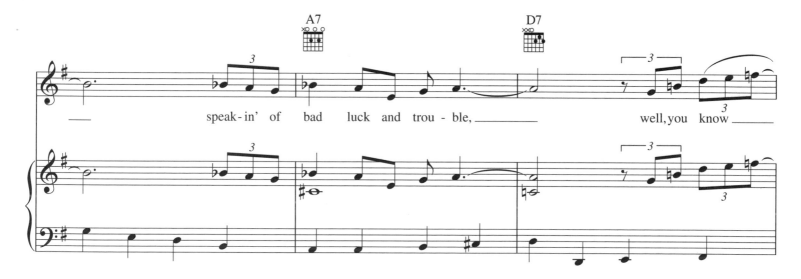

__ speak-in' of bad luck and trou - ble, _____ well, you know _____

I've my share. Ev-'ry

D.S. al Coda

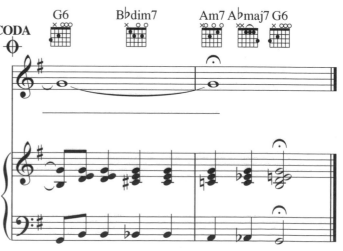

CODA

GOOD BAIT

By TADD DAMERON
and COUNT BASIE

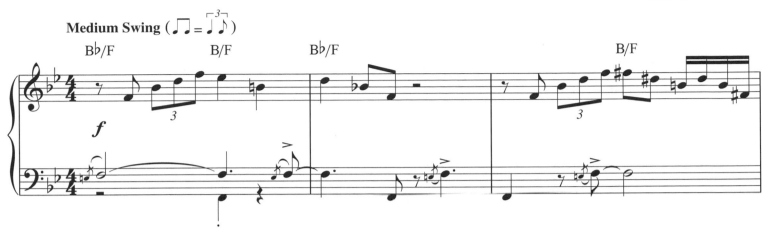

26

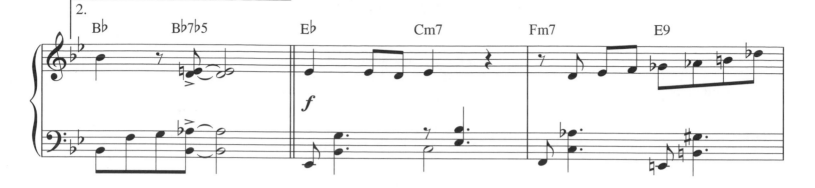

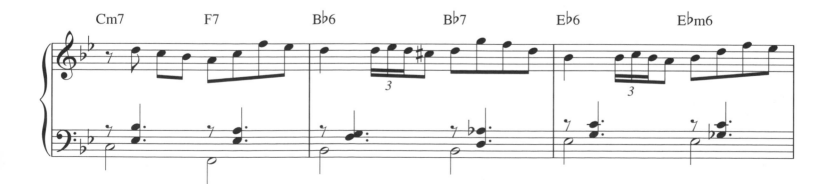

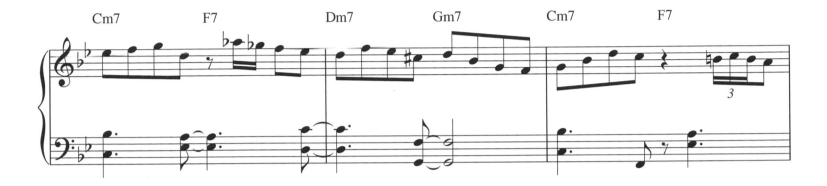

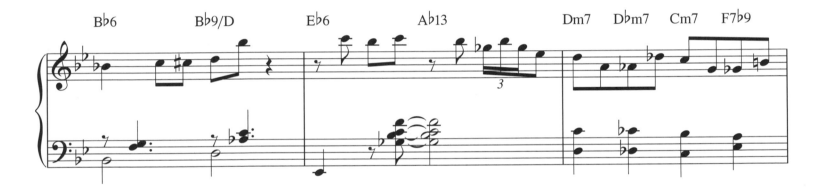

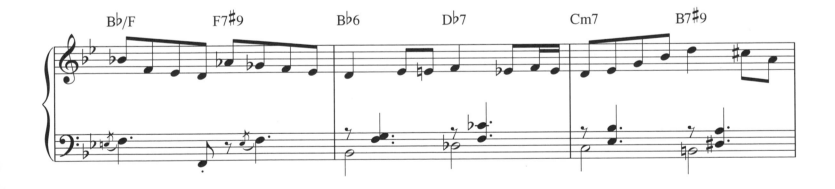

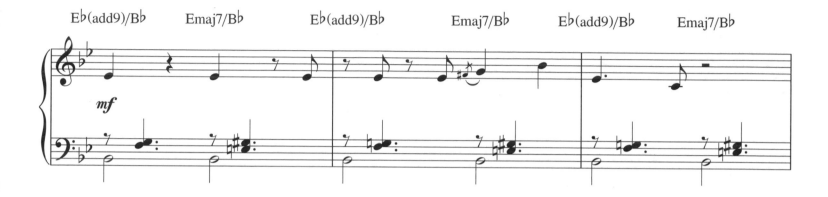

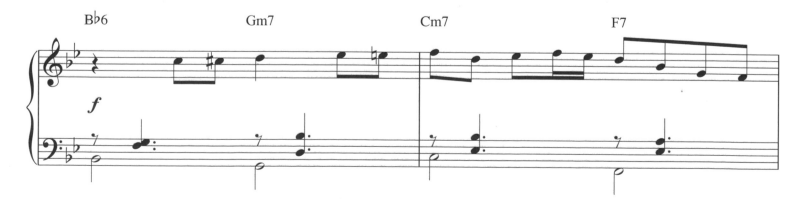

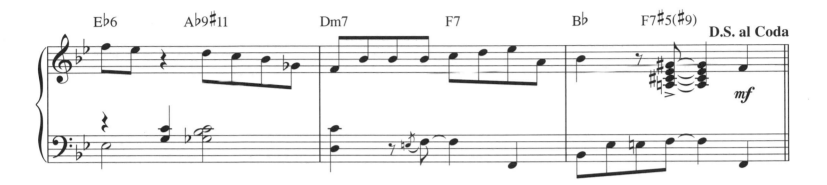

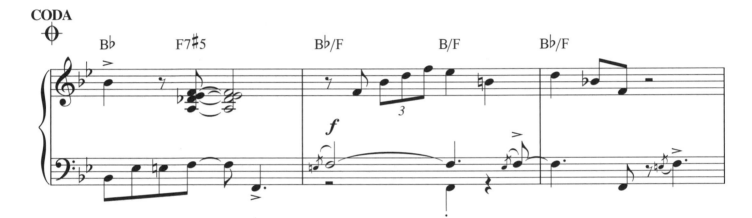

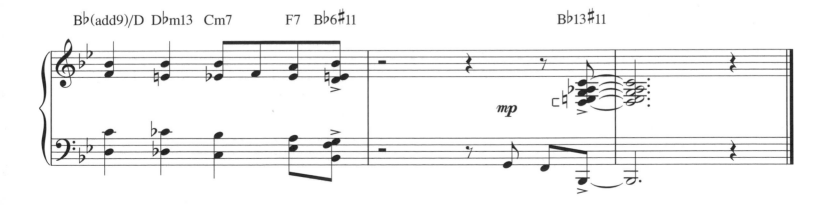

GOOD MORNING BLUES

By COUNT BASIE,
JIMMIE RUSHING, and ED DURHAM

Lyrics:
Good morn-ing blues; blues, how do ___ you do? ___
Good morn - ing blues; blues, how do ___ you do? _
Babe, I feel all right, _ but I

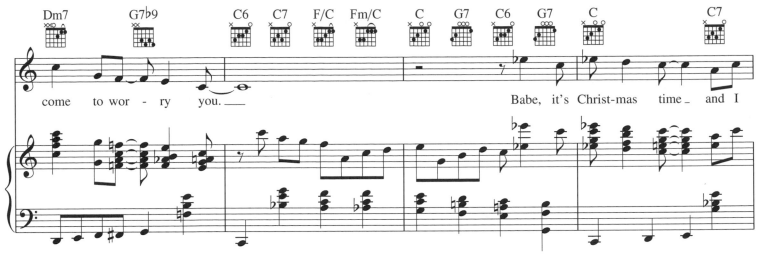

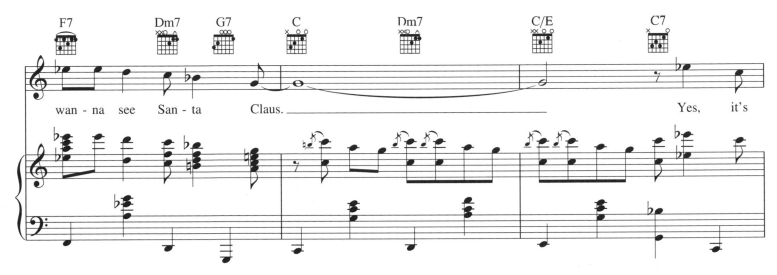

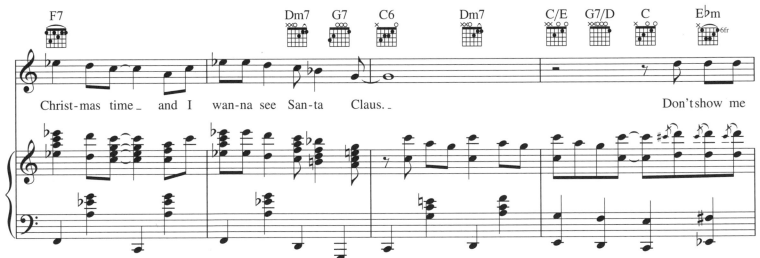

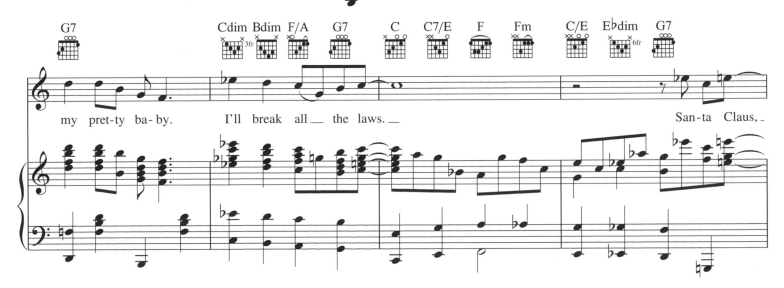

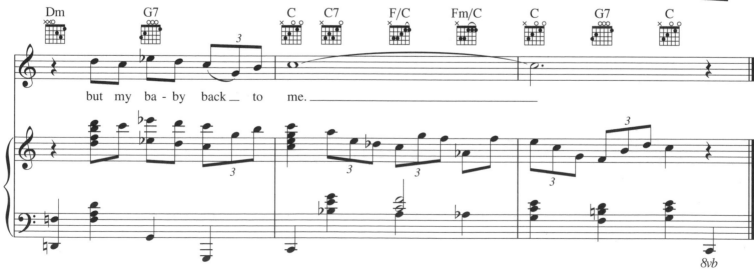

8vb

LESTER LEAPS IN

By LESTER YOUNG

Fast Swing

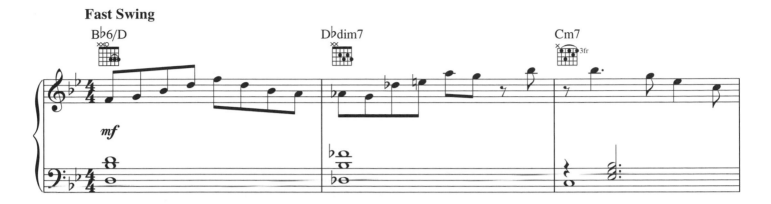

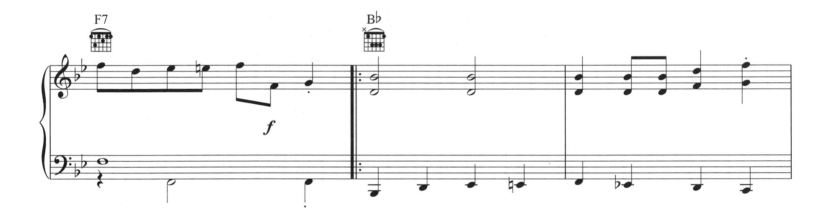

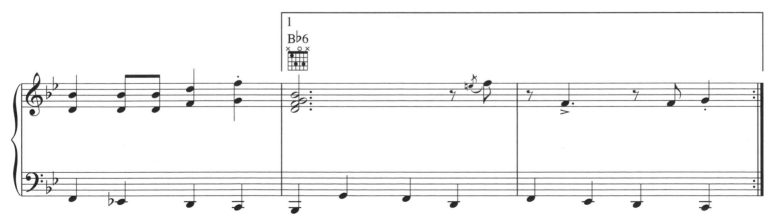

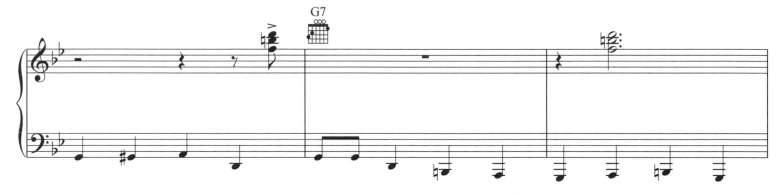

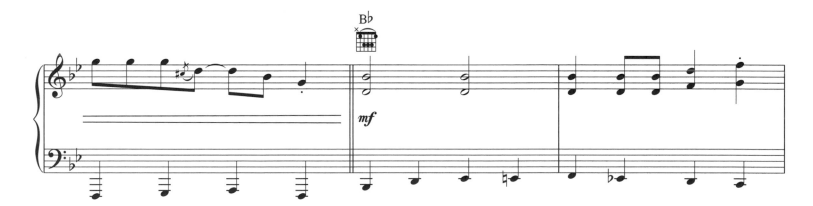

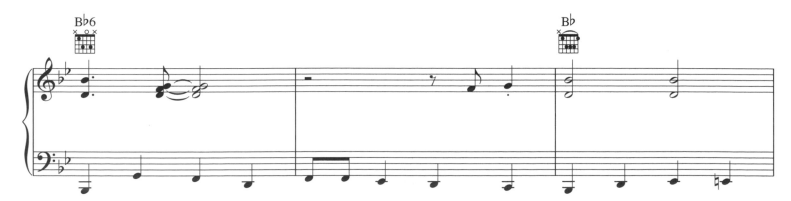

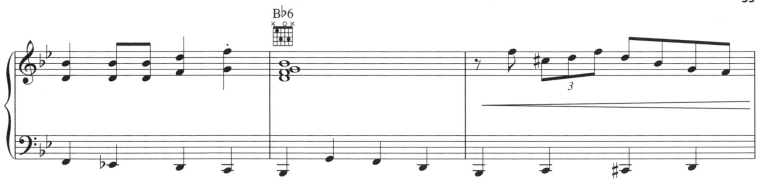

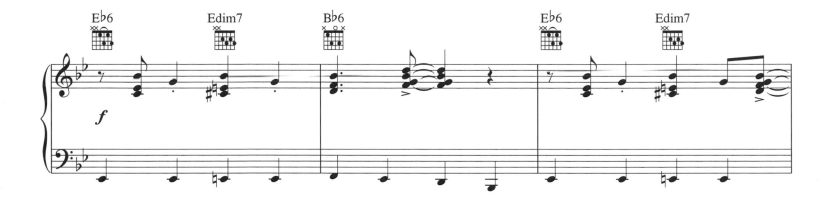

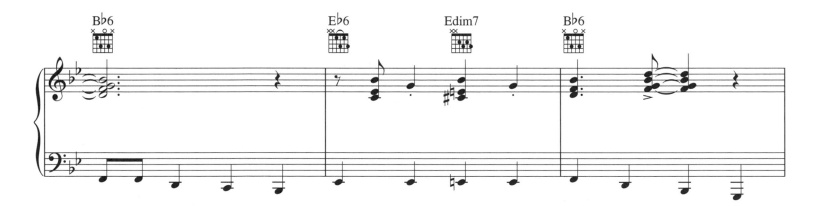

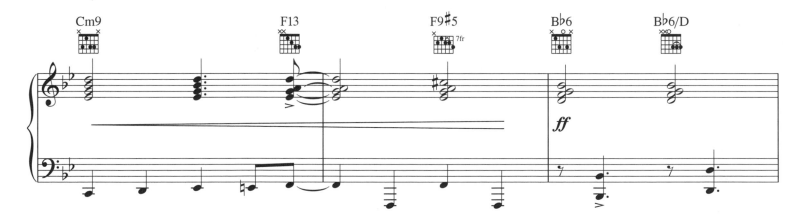

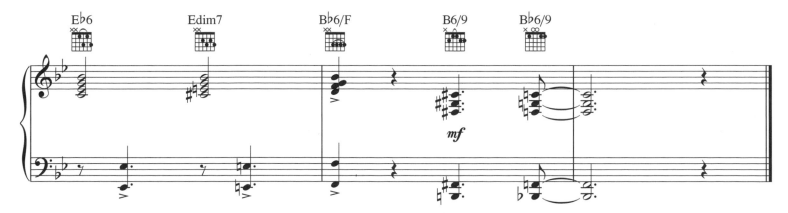

I NEVER KNEW

Words by GUS KAHN
Music by TED FIORITO

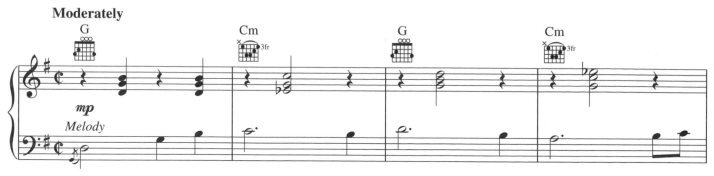

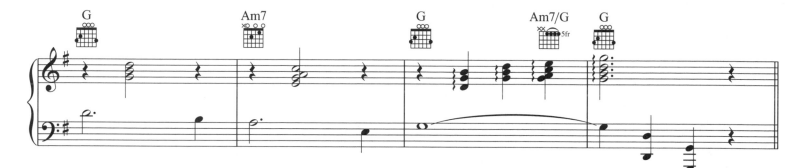

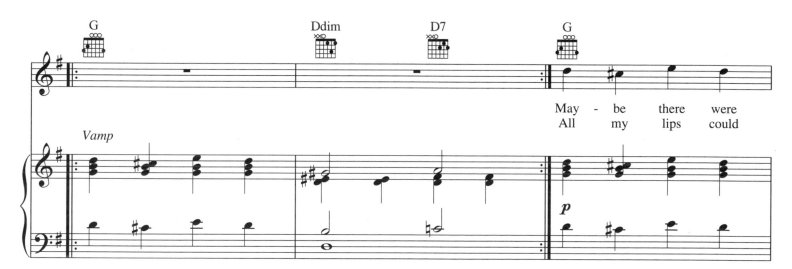

May - be there were
All my there lips could

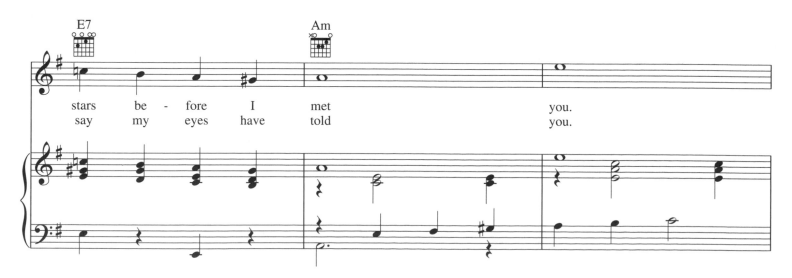

stars be - fore I met you.
say my eyes have told you.

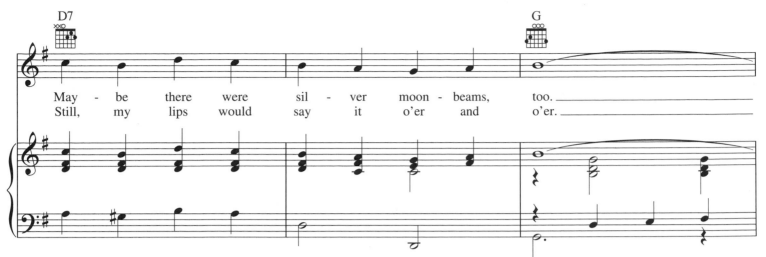

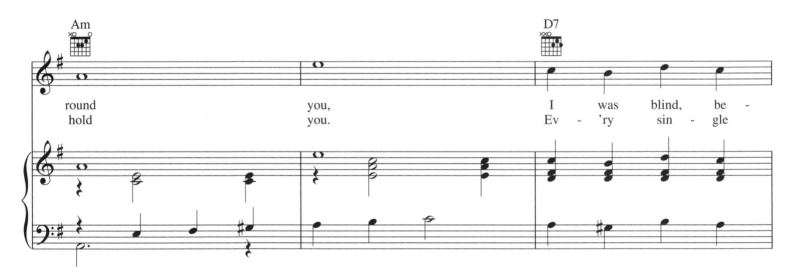

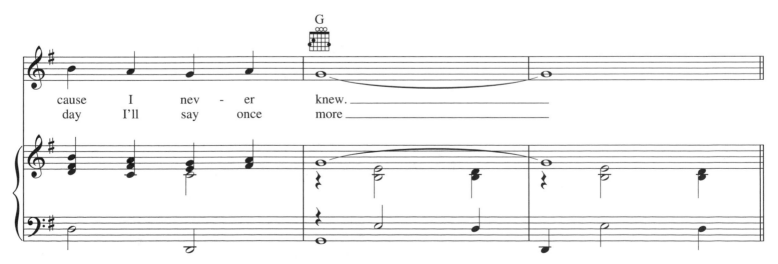

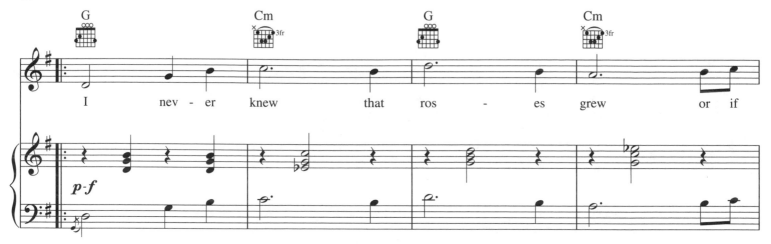

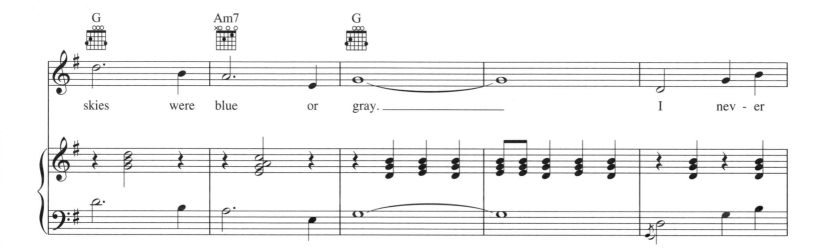

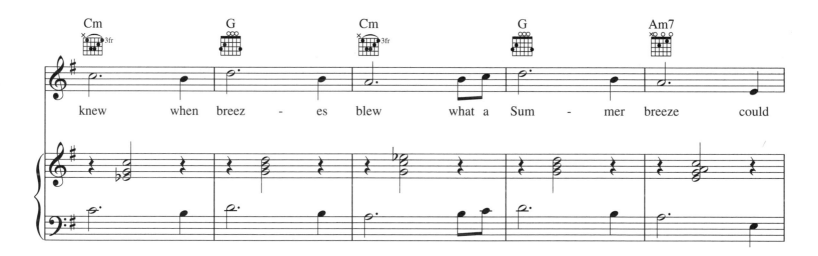

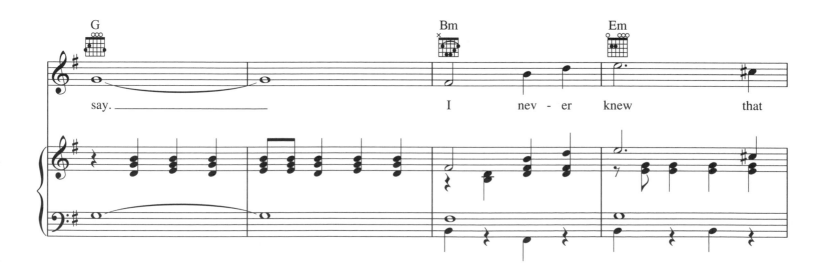

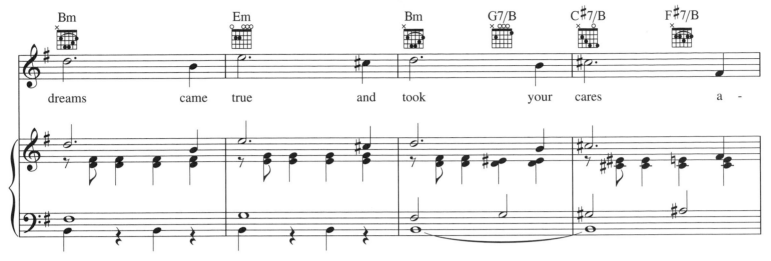

dreams came true and took your cares a-

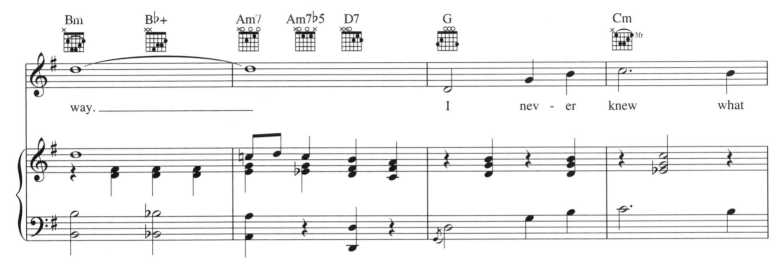

way. _____ I nev-er knew what

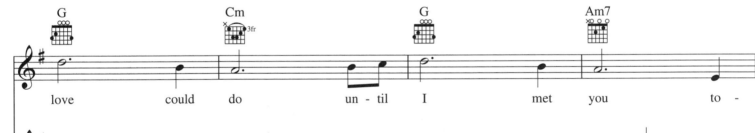

love could do un-til I met you to-

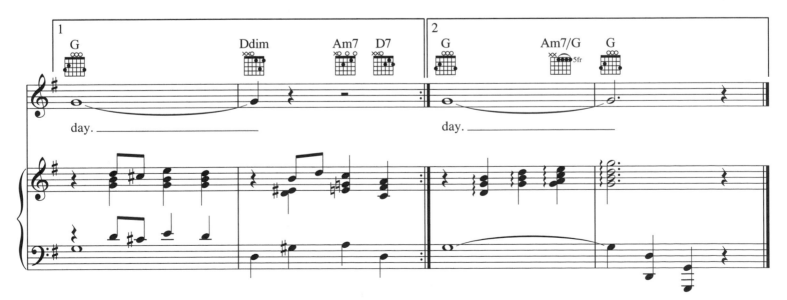

day. _____ day. _____

JIVE AT FIVE

By COUNT BASIE
and HARRY "SWEETS" EDISON

Jump tempo

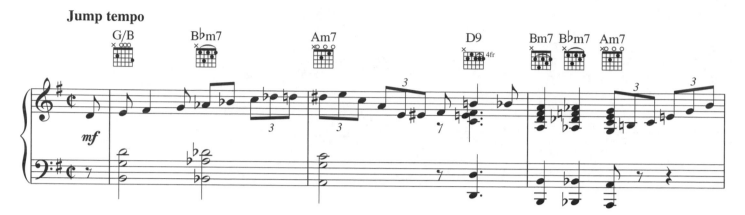

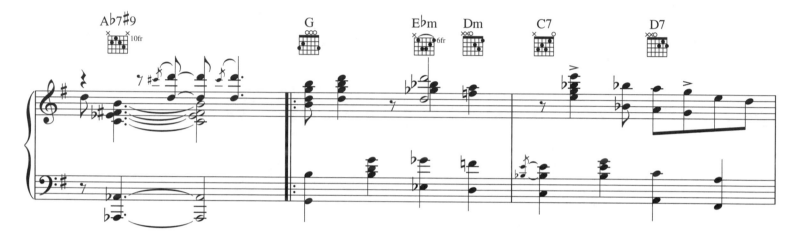

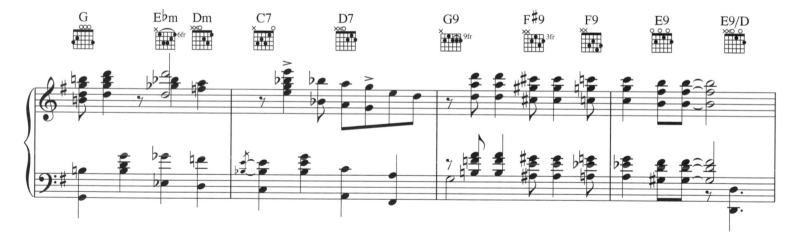

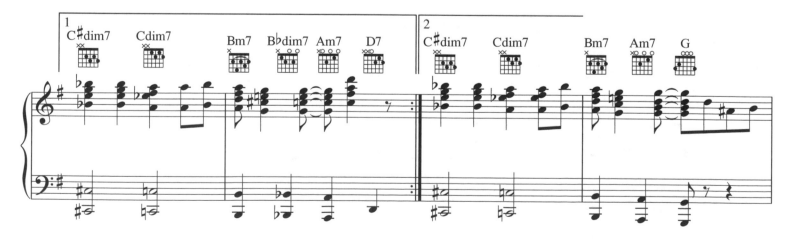

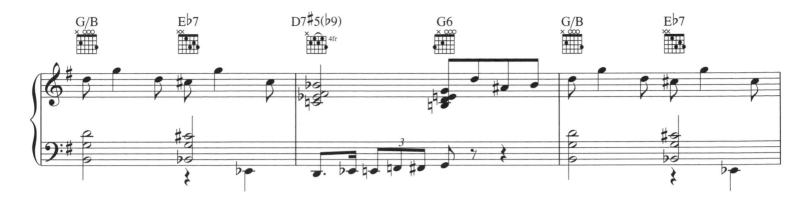

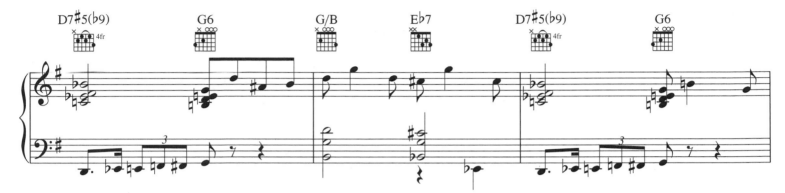

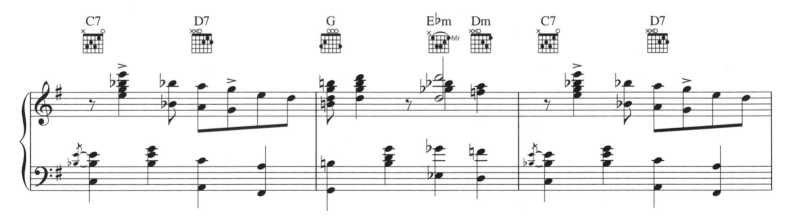

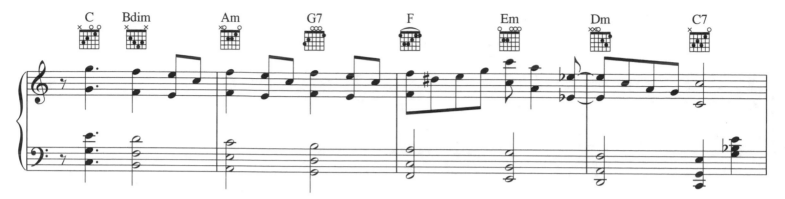

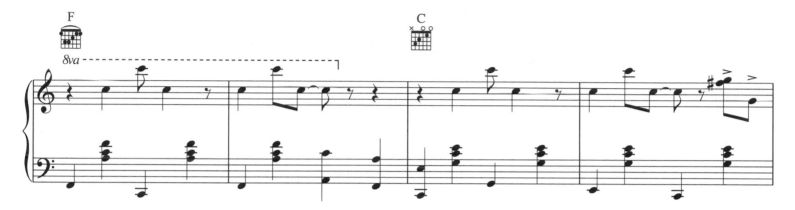

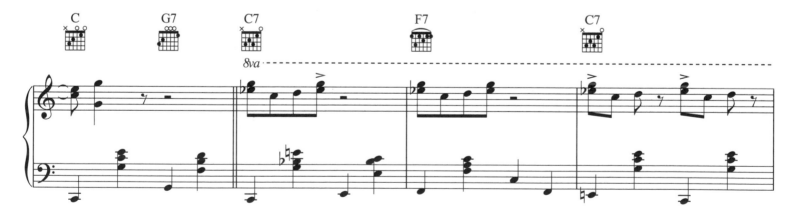

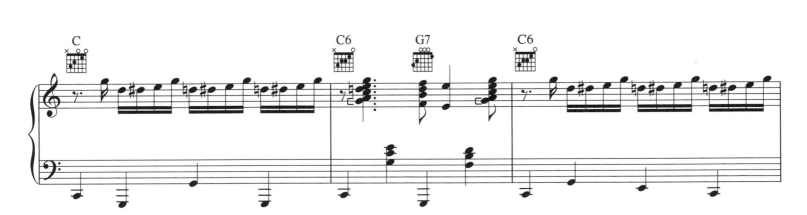

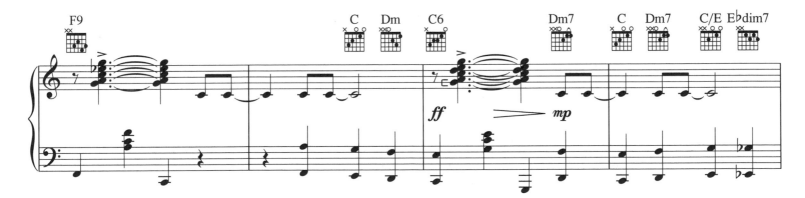

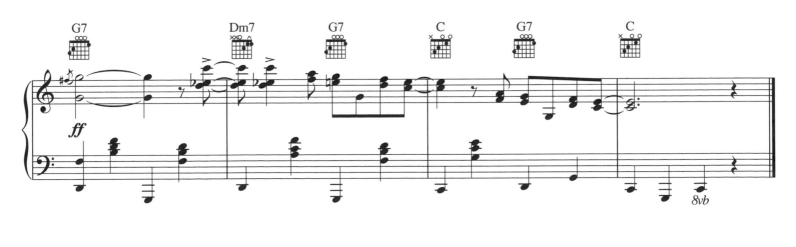

JUMPIN' AT THE WOODSIDE

Music by COUNT BASIE
Words by JON HENDRICKS

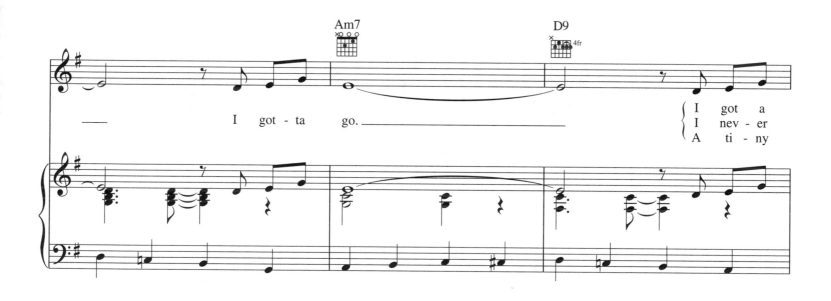

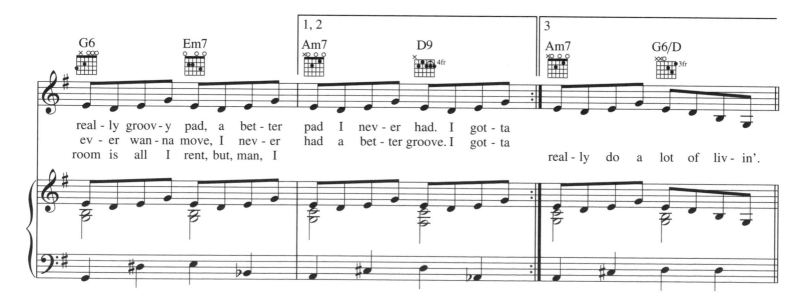

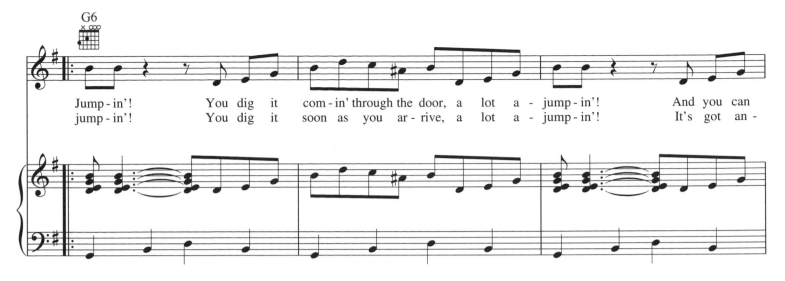

Jump-in'! You dig it com-in' through the door, a lot a - jump-in'! And you can
jump-in'! You dig it soon as you ar-rive, a lot a - jump-in'! It's got an -

feel the shak-in' floor, a lot of jump-in'! And you'll be com-in' back for more. I tell you
oth-er kind of jive, a lot of jump-in'! And real-ly ver-y much a-live. I tell you

jump-in', man, they're jump-in' at the Wood-side now. A lot a Wood-side now!

LI'L DARLIN'

By NEAL HEFTI

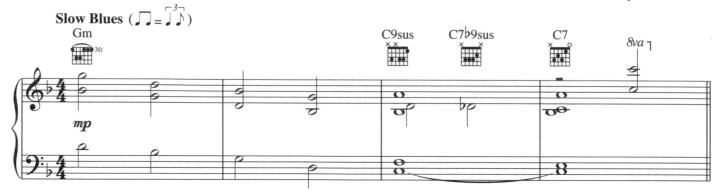

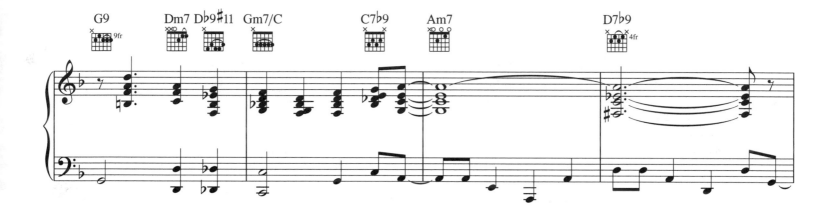

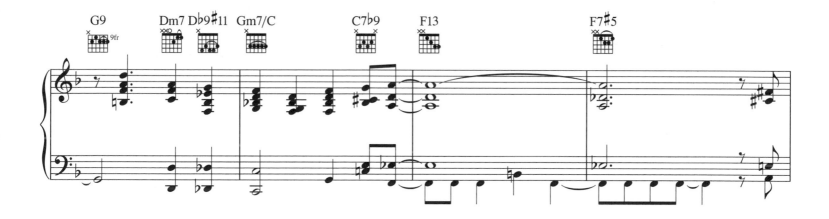

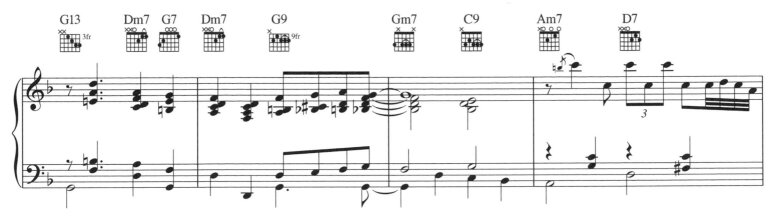

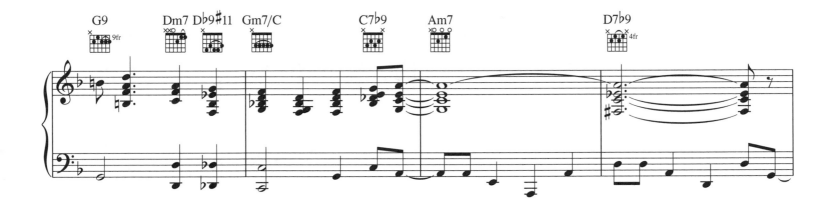

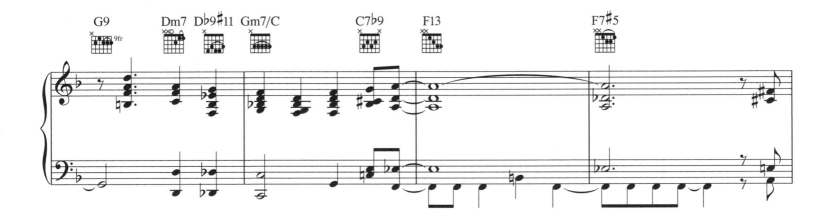

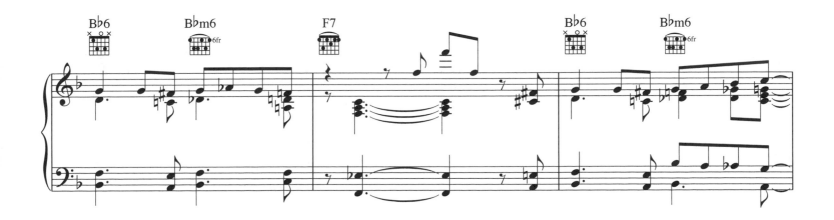

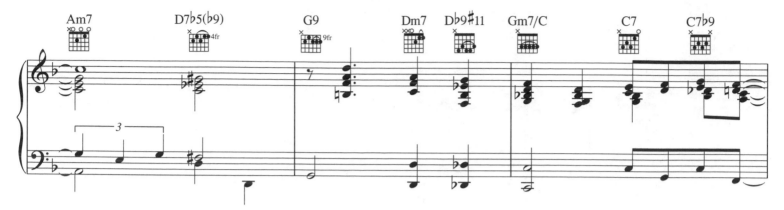

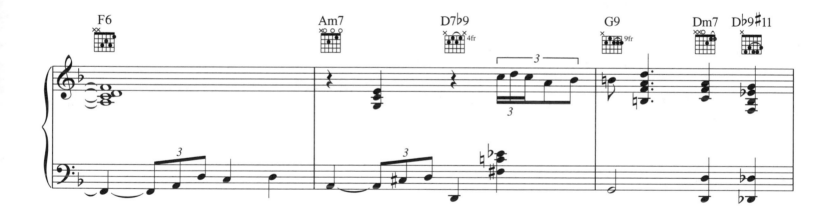

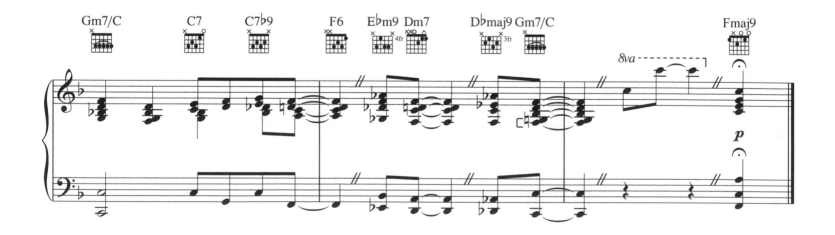

SHINY STOCKINGS

Words by ELLA FITZGERALD
Music by FRANK FOSTER

when we go to a dance? __ Oh, no, __
do I think of ro - mance? __ No, all __

__ you take a glance __ at those shin -
__ I do is glance __ at those shin -

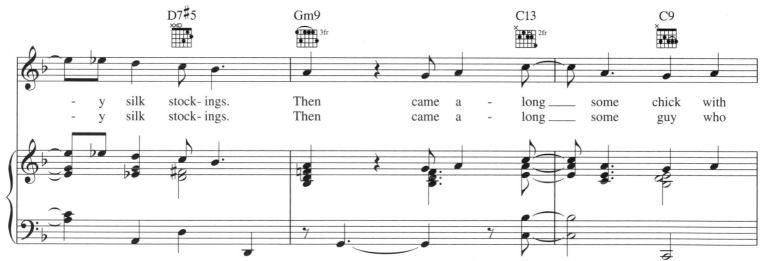

- y silk stock - ings. Then came a - long __ some chick with
- y silk stock - ings. Then came a - long __ some guy who

great big stock - ings, too, __ when you changed your mind _
dug your stock - ings, too, __ when you changed your mind _

ONE MINT JULEP

By RUDOLPH TOOMBS

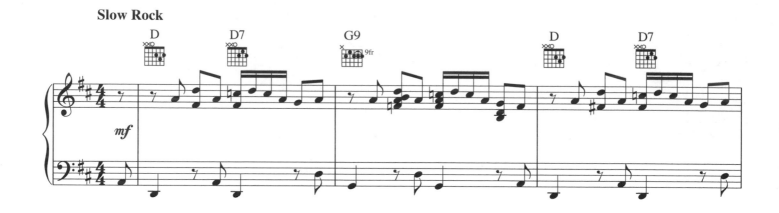

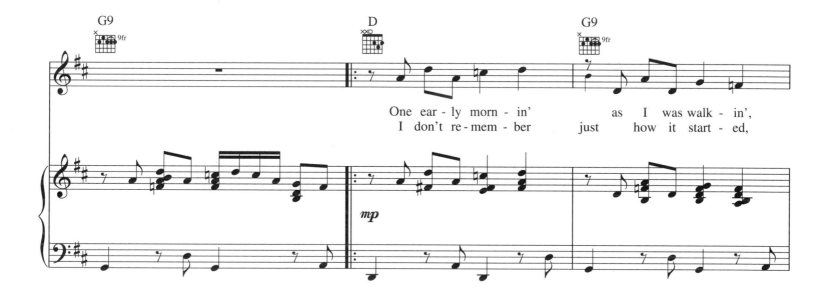

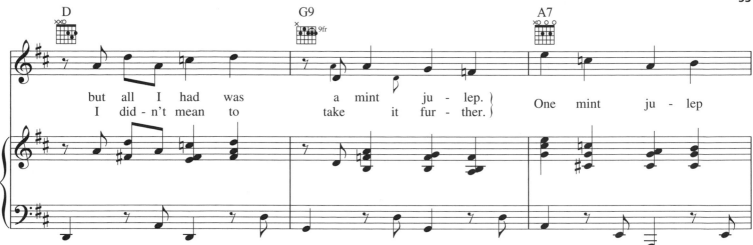

but all I had was a mint ju - lep.)
I did - n't mean to take it fur - ther.) One mint ju - lep

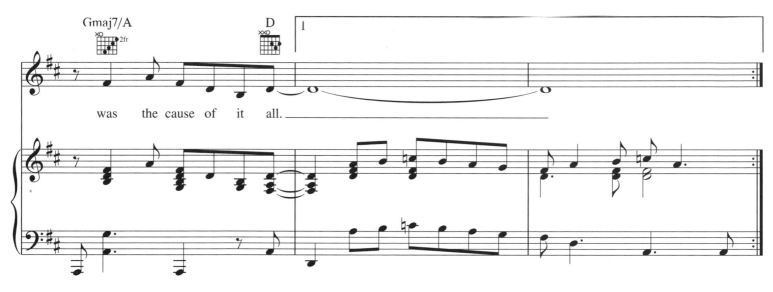

was the cause of it all.

The lights were burn-ing low there in the tav-ern, when

through the swing-in' door up popped her fa - ther. He said, "I saw you when

you kissed my daugh-ter. Got to wed her right now, or face a slaugh-ter."

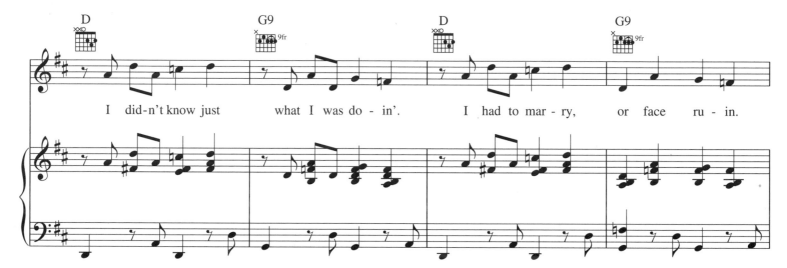

I did-n't know just what I was do-in'. I had to mar-ry, or face ru-in.

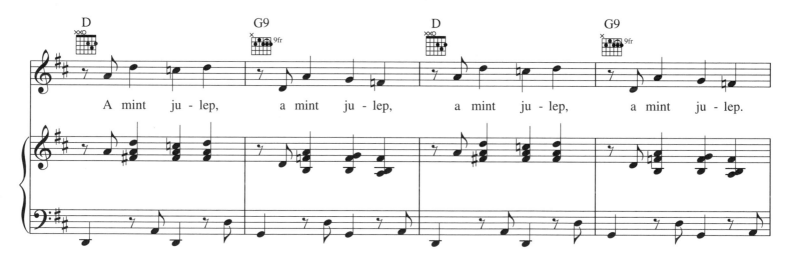

A mint ju-lep, a mint ju-lep, a mint ju-lep, a mint ju-lep.

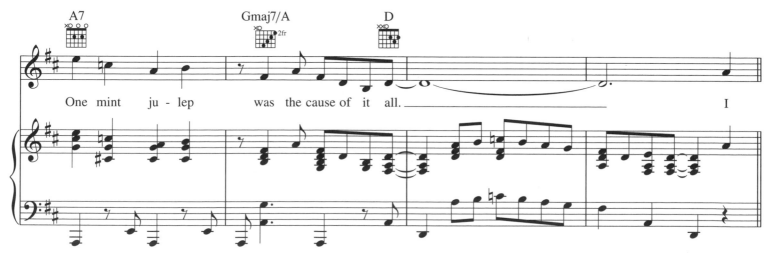

One mint ju-lep was the cause of it all. _____ I

don't want to bore you with my trou-ble, but from now on I'll be think - ing dou-ble. I'll

buy her ros-es or may - be tu-lips. I got too much trou-ble from _ buy-ing ju - leps.

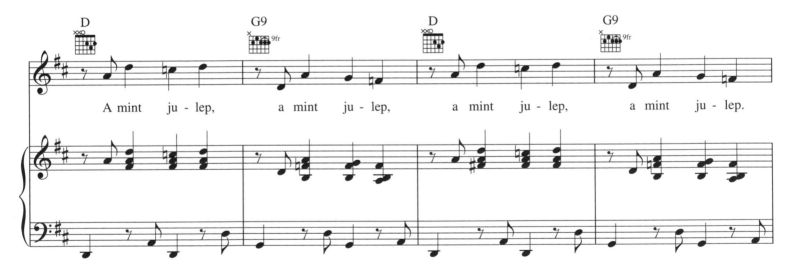

A mint ju - lep, a mint ju - lep, a mint ju - lep, a mint ju - lep.

One mint ju - lep was the cause of it all. _____

ONE O'CLOCK JUMP

By COUNT BASIE

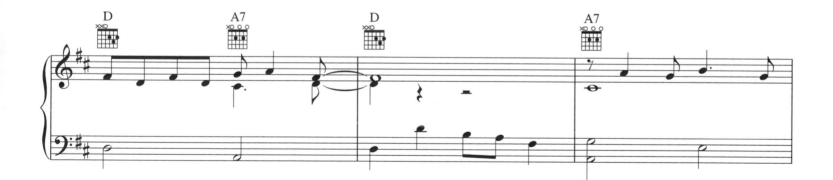

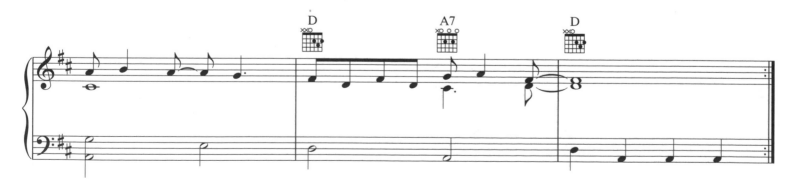

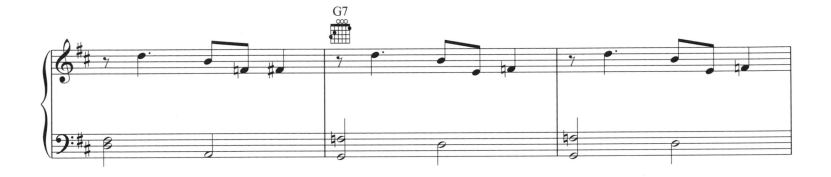

POOR BUTTERFLY

Words by JOHN L. GOLDEN
Music by RAYMOND HUBBELL

There's a sto - ry told of a lit - tle Jap - a - nese
"Won't you tell my love," she would whis - per to the breeze,

dreamily

sit - ting de - mure - ly 'neath the cher - ry blos - soms trees.
"tell him I'm wait - ing 'neath the cher - ry blos - som trees,

Miss But - ter - fly her
my sail - or man to

name. _____ A sweet lit - tle in - no - cent child was she, till a
see. _____ The bees and the hum - ming - birds say they guess, ev'ry

SHE'S FUNNY THAT WAY

Words by RICHARD A. WHITING
Music by NEIL MORET

SWEET GEORGIA BROWN

Words and Music by BEN BERNIE,
MACEO PINKARD and KENNETH CASEY

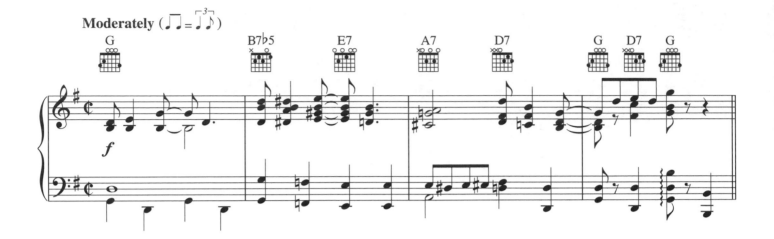

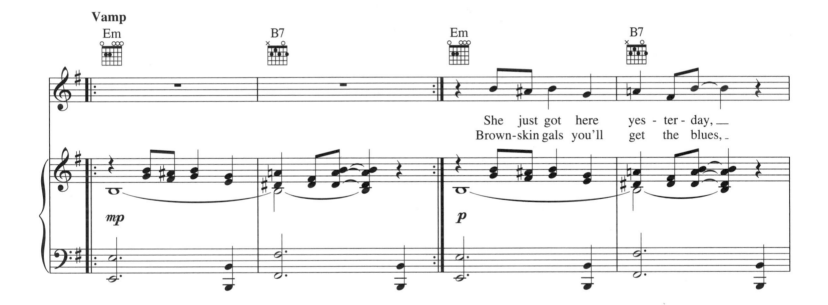

no gal made⁓ } has got a shade⁓ on Sweet Geor-gia Brown.⁓
No gal made⁓ }

Two left feet,⁓ but oh so neat,⁓ has Sweet Geor-gia Brown.⁓

They all sigh⁓ and wan-na die⁓ for Sweet Geor-gia Brown.⁓ I'll tell⁓ you just

why,⎯⎯⎯⎯⎯⎯⎯ you know⁓ I don't lie, *(spoken ad lib.)* not much!

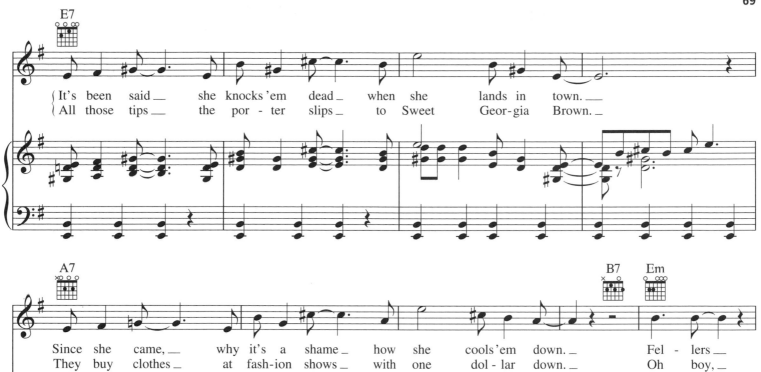

It's been said __ she knocks 'em dead __ when she lands in town. __
All those tips __ the por-ter slips __ to Sweet Geor-gia Brown. __

Since she came, __ why it's a shame __ how she cools 'em down. __ Fel-lers __
They buy clothes __ at fash-ion shows __ with one dol-lar down. __ Oh boy, __

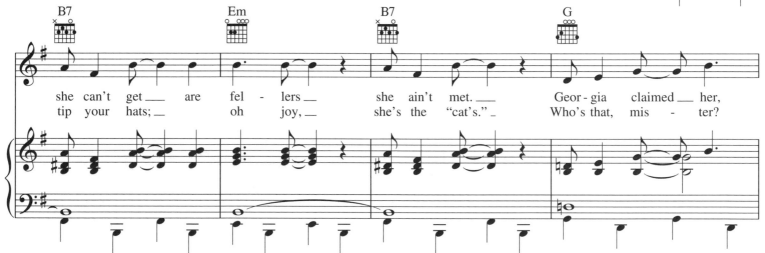

she can't get __ are fel-lers __ she ain't met. __ Geor-gia claimed __ her,
tip your hats; __ oh joy, __ she's the "cat's." __ Who's that, mis - ter?

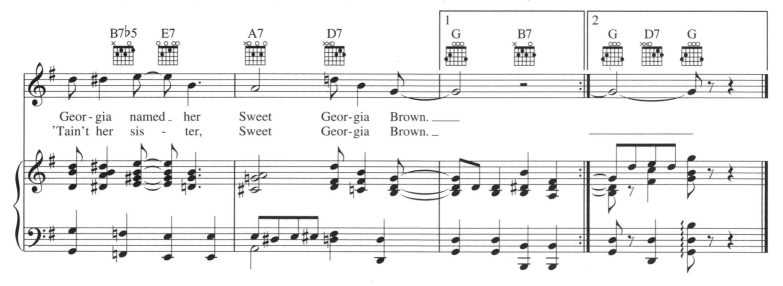

Geor-gia named __ her Sweet Geor-gia Brown. __
'Tain't her sis - ter, Sweet Geor-gia Brown. __

SWINGIN' THE BLUES

By COUNT BASIE
and EDDIE DURHAM

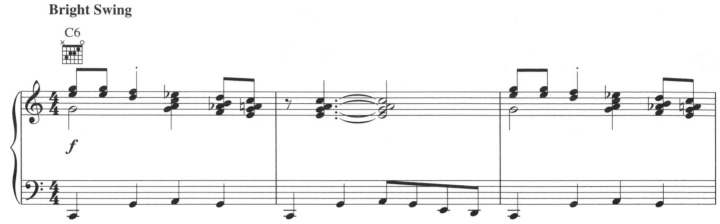

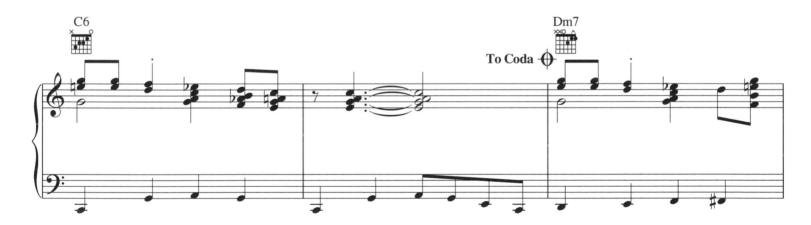

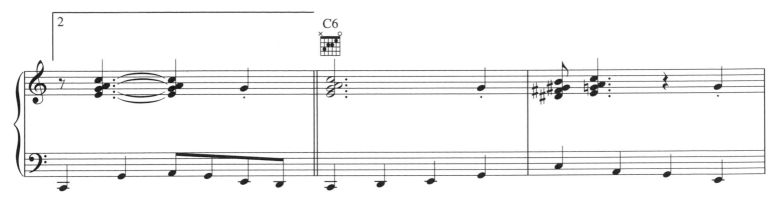

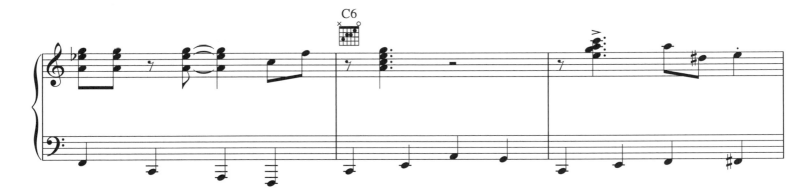

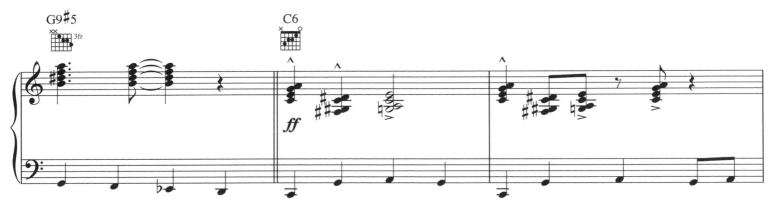

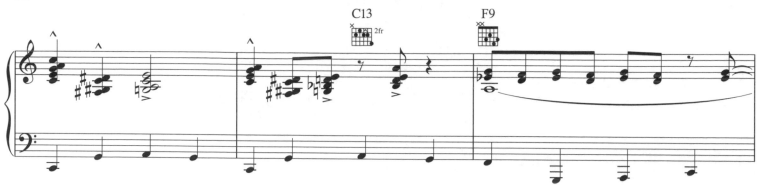

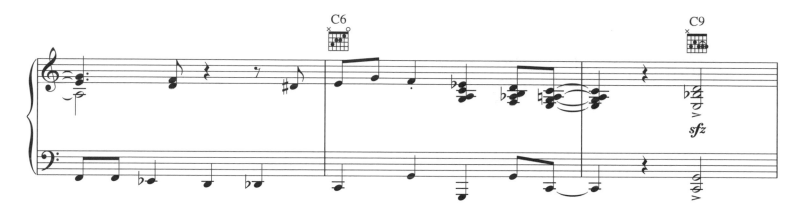

D.C. al Coda

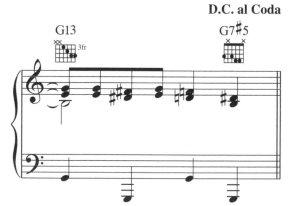

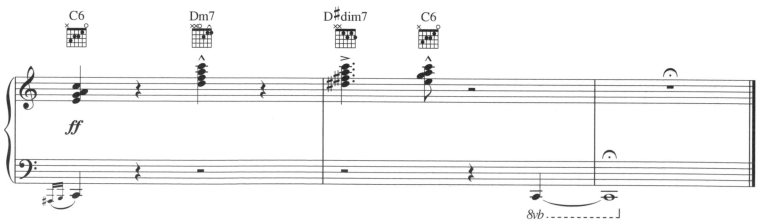

TOPSY

Written by EDGAR BATTLE
and EDDIE DURHAM

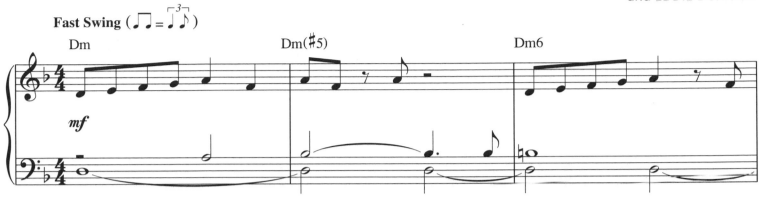

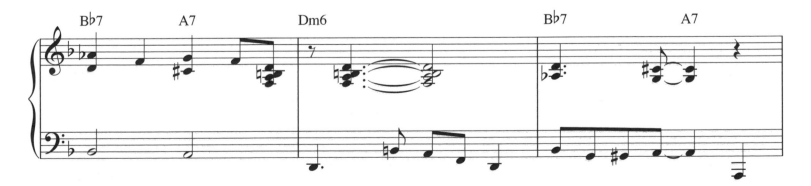

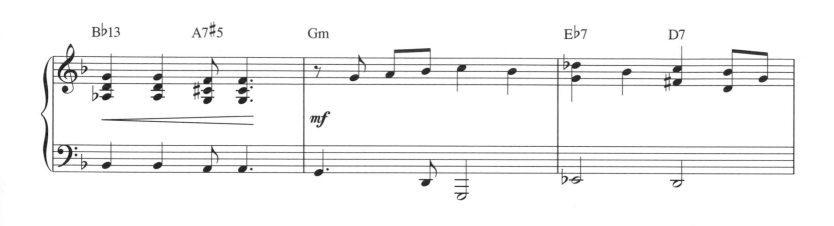

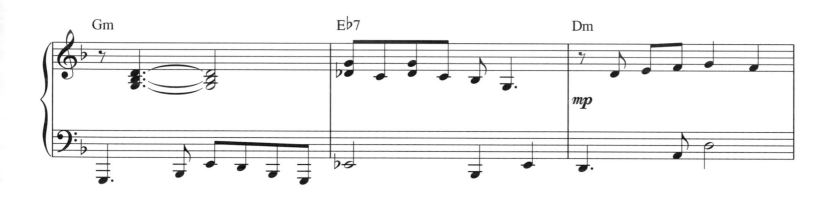

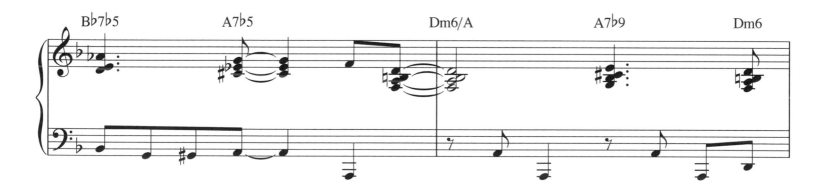

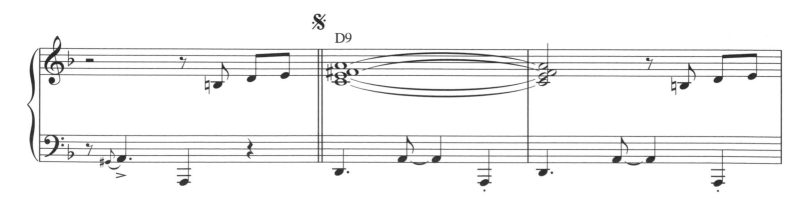

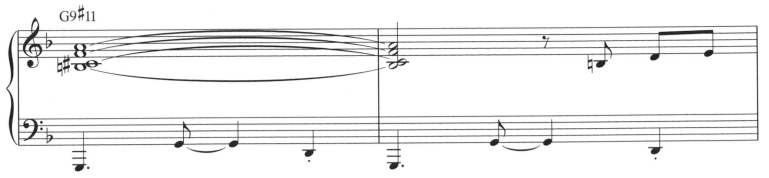

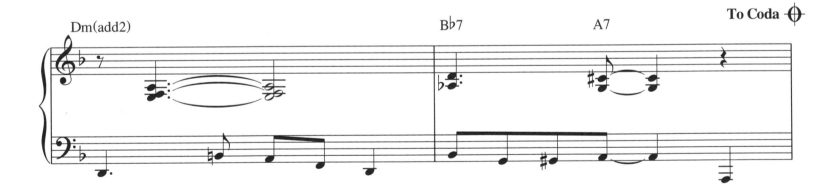

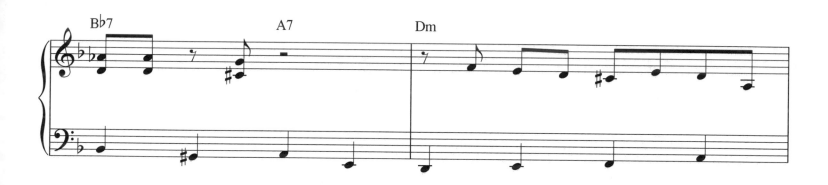

UNTIL I MET YOU
(Corner Pocket)

Words and Music by FREDDIE GREEN
and DON WOLF

Medium Swing

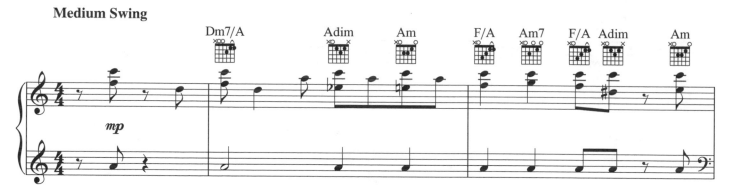

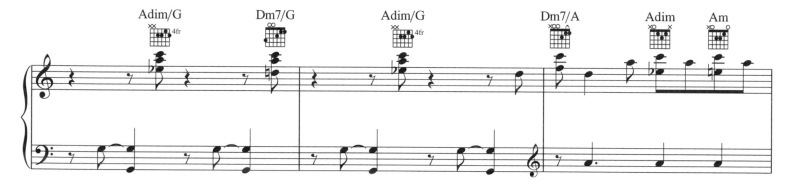

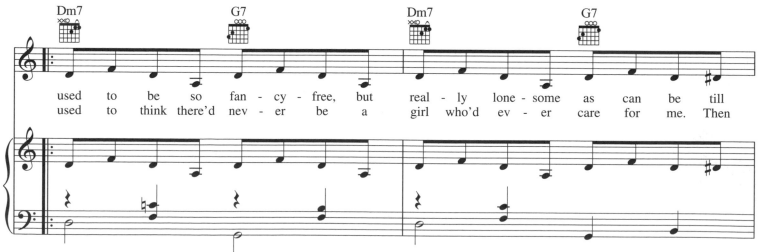

used to be so fan-cy-free, but real-ly lone-some as can be till

used to think there'd nev-er be a girl who'd ev-er care for me. Then